Designer Dogs

Yochons

by Ruth Owen

PowerKiDS press
New York

Published in 2015 by The Rosen Publishing Group, Inc.
29 East 21st Street, New York, NY 10010

First Edition

Produced for Rosen by Ruby Tuesday Books Ltd
Editor for Ruby Tuesday Books Ltd: Mark J. Sachner
US Editor: Joshua Shadowens
Designer: Emma Randall

Photo Credits:
Cover, 1, 3, 4 (right), 5, 6, 19, 20–21, 22–23, 25, 26–27, 29, 30 © Warren Photographic; 4 (left), 4 (center), 7, 8–9, 10–11, 12–13, 14–15, 21 (top) © Shutterstock; 16, 18 © Etherd & Diane Blake; 17 © Getty Images; 28 © Corbis.

Library of Congress Cataloging-in-Publication Data

Owen, Ruth, 1967– author.
Yochons / by Ruth Owen. — First edition.
pages cm. — (Designer dogs)
Includes index.
ISBN 978-1-4777-7043-6 (library binding) — ISBN 978-1-4777-7044-3 (pbk.) —
ISBN 978-1-4777-7045-0 (6-pack)
1. Yo Chon—Juvenile literature. 2. Toy dogs—Juvenile literature. 3. Dogs—Juvenile literature. I. Title.
SF429.Y55O94 2015
636.76—dc23

2014006011

Manufactured in the United States of America

CPSIA Compliance Information: Batch #WS14PK8: For Further Information contact Rosen Publishing, New York, New York at 1-800-237-9932

Contents

Meet a Yochon 4
Designer Yochons 6
Meet the Parents: Yorkshire Terriers 8
Meet the Parents: Glamorous Yorkies.............10
Meet the Parents: Bichon Frise.........................12
Meet the Parents: Sailor Pups 14
Gorgeous Yochons...16
Yochon Personalities 18
Yochon Puppies..20
Buying a Yochon Puppy 22
Waiting for Your Yochon..................................24
Comforting Your Pup..26
Your Yochon Goes to School 28
Glossary..30
Websites 31
Read More, Index..32

Meet a Yochon

What is tiny, has soft wavy hair, loves to clown around, and has tons of love to give? The answer is a yochon.

A yochon is a new kind of dog. Yochons are **crossbreed** dogs. A crossbreed dog is a cross, or mixture, of two different dog **breeds**. When a Yorkshire terrier and a Bichon Frise have puppies together, they make tiny, adorable yochons.

A crossbreed puppy can be more like one parent than the other in looks and personality. Sometimes it can be an equal mixture of both its parents' breeds.

Adult Yorkshire terrier

Adult Bichon Frise

Yochon puppy

The name "yochon" is made up from the words "Yorkshire" and "Bichon" in the names of the parent breeds. These dogs are also known as Yorkie-chons and Bichon Yorkies.

An eight-week-old yochon

Designer Yochons

Some breeds of dogs have been around for hundreds and even thousands of years! Yochons have been around for less than 20 years.

Yochons are not the only type of new crossbreed dog. In the past 20 to 30 years, dog **breeders** have been mixing lots of popular older dog breeds to create new types of dogs.

These new crossbreed dogs are known as designer dogs because people have designed, or created, them.

A yochon puppy

Here are some of the designer dog breeds that people have created.

Cavachons = cavalier King Charles spaniels + Bichon Frises

Goldendoodles = golden retrievers + poodles

Puggles = pugs + beagles

Yorkipoos = Yorkshire terriers + poodles

A cavachon puppy

An adult goldendoodle

A yorkipoo puppy

An adult puggle

Meet the Parents: Yorkshire Terriers

Today, most Yorkshire terriers live as pet dogs. Their job is to be loving **companions** to their owners.

The **ancestors** of today's Yorkshire terriers were working dogs, however. In the 1800s, Yorkshire terriers worked as rat catchers in mills that made clothing and other products from cotton and wool. The breed gets its name from the English county of Yorkshire, where the dogs were first bred.

There are many different terrier dog breeds. Terrier breeds were created by people for catching animals such as foxes, rabbits, and rats. These tough, small breeds were even bred to dive into the underground burrows of the animals they hunted.

Yorkshire terrier puppies

A Yorkshire terrier

Meet the Parents: Glamorous Yorkies

With their long, silky golden-brown and steel-blue coats **groomed** and a bow in their hair, Yorkies are the glamour guys and gals of the dog world.

These **feisty**, energetic little dogs haven't forgotten their history, though. Their days as rat-catchers may be over, but they still love to use their terrier skills to hunt for toys. And if a squirrel dares to enter a Yorkie's backyard, it will soon be chased away!

Adult Yorkshire terrier size

Height to shoulder:
8 to 9 inches (20–23 cm)

An adult Yorkshire terrier usually weighs less than 7 pounds (3 kg).

A Yorkie with a long coat

This Yorkie's coat has been clipped, or trimmed.

Meet the Parents: Bichon Frise

Just like Yorkshire terriers, Bichon Frise, or Bichons, are bred to be companion dogs to people. These little dogs are smart, bubbly, and very cheerful.

Bichons adore their owners and need to be with them as much as possible. If you own a Bichon, you can't leave him or her home alone for long periods of time because the little dog will become anxious and unhappy.

A Bichon's thick, curly coat needs lots of attention. It must be groomed every day to remove tangles. Regular baths are also needed to keep the white hair clean.

Adult Bichon Frise size

Height to shoulder = up to 11.5 inches (29 cm)

Many Bichon owners take their pets to a dog beauty parlor every four to six weeks. A dog groomer bathes the dog, trims its hair and nails, and cleans inside its ears.

A Bichon Frise gets a haircut from a dog groomer

Meet the Parents: Sailor Pups

The Bichon Frise breed has been around for centuries. It's believed the dogs were first bred in countries around the Mediterranean Sea.

Hundreds of years ago, Bichon Frise sailed the seas of Europe as the pets of Spanish and Italian sailors. The dogs were so popular that their owners could barter, or swap, them for goods on their voyages.

In the 1300s, this breed became popular with wealthy people and royal families in European countries such as Italy and Spain. In the 1500s, the dogs became popular in France.

A mother Bichon and her puppies

An old **legend** says that King Henry III of France carried his Bichons everywhere he went. The little dogs rode in a basket that was hung around the king's neck.

Gorgeous Yochons

With its glamorous mom and dad, you can be sure that a yochon is going to be gorgeous!

Like their parent breeds, yochons are very small dogs. When fully grown, a yochon is usually less than 1 foot (30 cm) tall. An adult yochon weighs less than 10 pounds (4.5 kg).

A yochon's hair can be a single solid color such as black, white, or tan. It might also have a coat that includes more than one color, for example white, tan, and silvery-gray.

An adult yochon

A yochon's coat is very soft, and usually has a slight wave through it.

Yochon Personalities

A yochon's main job in life is to give love to its human family. Lots and lots of love!

Yochons are bred to be lap dogs. A lap dog is a small dog that can fit on a person's lap and loves to spend time cuddled up close to its owner.

While cuddling on the sofa is a favorite pastime, yochons do have lots of energy to burn off. These energetic little dogs need to be walked every day. A yochon will also enjoy time off its leash playing games with its owner in a yard or other safe space.

An adult yochon

Yochons need to be with their owners as much as possible. They will become unhappy if they are left alone all day while their human family is at school or work.

A yochon puppy playing with his kitty pal

Yochon Puppies

A yochon puppy may have a Yorkshire terrier mom and a Bichon Frise dad. In some yochon families it's the other way around. The mother dog gives birth to about five yochon puppies at one time.

Like all newborn pups, yochons spend nearly all their time sleeping. They snuggle up to their mother's warm, furry body. When mom takes a break to get some food or exercise, the little pups cuddle up to each other in a tangled heap.

Mom Bichon Frise

Dad Yorkshire Terrier

A newborn yochon pup is teeny tiny. It weighs just 5 ounces (142 g). It measures 4 inches (10 cm) from its bottom to its tiny black nose.

Yochon puppies

Buying a Yochon Puppy

If you want to own a yochon, your family will need to find a breeder. Always choose a breeder who raises puppies in his or her home. A good breeder should play with the puppies and give them lots of love.

Puppies raised in a loving home will know what it's like to be part of a human family. They will grow up knowing that people are friends. Don't buy a puppy from a pet store. These puppies have often been raised in cages and have not gotten used to people.

Once the yochon puppies are about four to five weeks old, ask the breeder if you can visit the puppies to choose which one will be your new dog.

When you visit a breeder's house, always ask if you can meet the mom dog. Check that mom is a friendly, confident, happy dog. If mom has a nice nature, hopefully her pups will, too.

These yochon pups
are six weeks old.

Waiting for Your Yochon

You won't be able to take your puppy home right away. Like all puppies, your little yochon must spend its first few weeks with its dog family.

Your yochon puppy will grow big and healthy feeding on its mother's **nutritious** milk. It will get stronger and gain confidence by play fighting and chasing with its brothers and sisters.

When your yochon puppy is eight weeks old, it will be ready to leave its mom and come live with you.

Good breeders may have a list of people waiting for a puppy. If people are willing to go on a waiting list, it shows they are serious about owning a dog and are not making a quick decision.

Comforting Your Pup

One great way to prepare your new pup for the big changes ahead is to leave a T-shirt at the breeders that has your smell on it. Your puppy can sleep on the T-shirt and play with it. Your puppy will get used to your smell and recognize you.

When you collect your puppy from the breeder's home, bring the T-shirt, too. The shirt will smell of the puppy's first home and doggie family. This will comfort the little pup on its first night away from its mom and brothers and sisters.

Your yochon puppy will start eating special canned puppy food when it is about four weeks old. Ask your breeder to give you some of this food to take home. Then your pup's first meals in your home will taste familiar.

Your Yochon Goes to School

You've made friends and learned lots at school. Your little yochon will, too. So sign him or her up for a puppy training class.

In puppy school, young dogs learn important commands such as "sit" and "stay." They spend time playing with other puppies, big and small, which teaches them good doggie manners. They learn that it's not OK to be **aggressive** or a bully.

Some puppy classes play "pass the puppy." The pups are passed from owner to owner. This gets young dogs used to being touched by strangers.

A puppy training class

A puppy learns more in its first 16 weeks than the rest of its life. Your yochon could be with you for 10 to 15 years, so it's important to give your dog a good start.

Glossary

aggressive (uh-GREH-siv) Ready or likely to attack.

ancestors (AN-ses-terz) Relatives who lived long ago.

breeders (BREE-derz) People who breed animals, such as dogs, and sell them.

breeds (BREEDZ) Different types of dogs. The word "breed" is also used to describe the act of mating two dogs in order for them to have puppies.

companions (kum-PAN-yunz) People or animals with whom one spends a lot of time.

crossbreed (KROS-breed) A type of dog created from two different breeds.

feisty (FY-stee) Lively, brave, and willing to take care of oneself.

groomed (GROOMD) Cleaned by brushing, washing, or licking.

legend (LEH-jend) A story handed down over the years that may be based on some facts but cannot be proven to be true.

nutritious (noo-TRIH-shus) Containing substances that a living thing needs to help it live and grow. Food and drink contains nutrients such as vitamins.

Websites

Due to the changing nature of Internet links, PowerKids Press has developed an online list of websites related to the subject of this book. This site is updated regularly. Please use this link to access the list:

www.powerkidslinks.com/ddog/yoch/

Read More

Dicker, Katie and Mike Saunders. *You Can Draw Dogs!* Draw Your Pet! New York: Gareth Stevens, 2013.

Graubart, Norman D. *My Dog*. Pets Are Awesome! New York: PowerKids Press, 2014.

Shores, Erika L. *All about Yorkshire Terriers*. Dogs, Dogs, Dogs. Mankato, MN: Capstone Press, 2013.

Index

B
Bichon Frise, 4–5, 12–13, 14–15, 20–21
breeders (of dogs), 6, 22, 24
breeds (of dogs), 4, 6, 8

C
cavachons, 6–7
companion dogs, 8, 12
crossbreeds, 4, 6

D
designer dogs, 6

F
feeding and food, 24, 26

G
goldendoodles, 6–7
grooming, 12–13

H
hair, 4, 10–11, 12–13, 17

K
King Henry III of France, 15

L
length of life, 29

M
Mediterranean Sea, 14
mother dogs, 20–21, 22

P
personalities, 4, 12, 18–19
puggles, 6–7
puppies, 4, 6–7, 9, 20–21, 22–23, 24–25, 26–27, 28–29
puppy training classes, 28

R
rats, 8

S
sailors, 14
sizes (of dogs), 4, 10–11, 16, 21

T
terriers, 8, 10

W
working dogs, 8

Y
yorkipoos, 6–7
Yorkshire, England, 8
Yorkshire terriers, 4–5, 8–9, 10–11, 12, 20–21